KRISHNA'S DIALOGUE
ON THE SOUL

KRISHNA'S DIALOGUE ON THE SOUL

TRANSLATED FROM THE SANSKRIT
WITH AN INTRODUCTION BY JUAN MASCARÓ

PENGUIN BOOKS

PENGUIN BOOKS

Published by the Penguin Group
Penguin Books Ltd, 27 Wrights Lane, London w8 5tz, England
Penguin Books USA Inc., 375 Hudson Street, New York, New York 10014, USA
Penguin Books Australia Ltd, Ringwood, Victoria, Australia
Penguin Books Canada Ltd, 10 Alcorn Avenue, Toronto, Ontario, Canada m4v 3b2
Penguin Books (NZ) Ltd, 182–190 Wairau Road, Auckland 10, New Zealand

Penguin Books Ltd, Registered Offices: Harmondsworth, Middlesex, England

These selections are from Juan Mascaró's translation of
The Bhagavad Gita, published in Penguin Classics 1962
This edition published 1995
1 3 5 7 9 10 8 6 4 2

Copyright ©Juan Mascaró, 1962
All rights reserved

Printed in England by Clays Ltd, St Ives plc

The *Bhagavad Gita* was included in the *Mahabharata*. This vast epic of over one hundred thousand slokas, or couplets, is the longest poem in the world: about thirty times as long as *Paradise Lost*, and about 140 times as long as the *Bhagavad Gita*!

The main story of the *Mahabharata* centres around forces of good and evil represented, on the whole, as the Pandavas and the Kuravas. The father of Dhrita-rashtra and Pandu was the king of Hastinapura about fifty miles north-east of modern Delhi. At his death Pandu succeeded to the throne, as his eldest brother, Dhrita-rashtra, was blind. The sons of Pandu were Yudhishthira, Bhima, Arjuna, Nakula, and Sahadeva. We find their names in the first chapter of the *Bhagavad Gita*. Dhrita-rashtra had one hundred sons and the eldest was Duryodhana, the incarnation of evil. Pandu died and the blind king Dhrita-rashtra brought up in his palace the five sons of his brother. The Pandavas became great warriors and Dhrita-rashtra appointed the eldest, Yudhishthira, as heir-apparent. This was the cause of the great rivalry and in the end of the great war.

The *Mahabharata* has eighteen books and the great battle where Duryodhana and all his enemies were destroyed lasted eighteen days. The *Bhagavad Gita* has eighteen chapters. There is no doubt that the war described in the *Mahabharata* is not symbolic and that it may even be based on historical fact; but the problem is different when we find the dialogue between Krishna and Arjuna set in a background of war. The *Mahabharata* is the growth of centuries and to include a story in the *Mahabharata* was a way of securing its immortality. We find in the vast poem the story later on developed in the *Ramayana*, the stories of Nala and Damayanti, Savitri, Sakuntala and king Dushyanta, and many others. The *Bhagavad Gita* is like a little shrine in a vast temple, a temple that is both a theatre and a fair of this world; and whilst the war in the *Mahabharata* may be meant as a real war it is obvious that the war in the *Bhagavad Gita* has a symbolic meaning. The Arjuna and Krishna that we find in the rest of the *Mahabharata* are different beings from the Krishna and Arjuna of the *Bhagavad Gita*. We find in the *Gita* that there is going to be a great battle for the rule of a Kingdom; and how can we doubt that this is the Kingdom of Heaven, the kingdom of the soul? Are we going to allow the forces of light in us or the forces of darkness to win? And yet, how easy not to fight, and to find reasons to withdraw from the battle! In the *Bhagavad Gita* Arjuna becomes the soul of man and Krishna the charioteer of the soul.

—From the Introduction by Juan Mascaró

The section represented here includes chapters ten to eighteen of the *Bhagavad Gita*.

Krishna's Dialogue on the Soul

10

KRISHNA

1 Hear again mighty Arjuna, hear the glory of my Word again. I speak for thy true good, because thy heart finds joy in me.

2 The hosts of the gods know not my birth, nor the great seers on earth, for all the gods come from me, and all the great seers, all.

3 He who knows I am beginningless, unborn, the Lord of all the worlds, this mortal is free from delusion, and from all evils he is free.

4 Intelligence, spiritual vision, victory over delusion,

5 patient forgiveness, truth, self-harmony, peacefulness, joys and sorrows, to be and not to be, fear and freedom from fear, harmlessness and non-violence, an ever-quietness, satisfaction, simple austerity, generosity, honour and dishonour: these are the conditions of mortals and they all arise from me.

6 The seven seers of times immemorial, and the four founders of the human race, being in me, came from my mind; and from them came this world of men.

7 He who knows my glory and power, he has the oneness of unwavering harmony. This is my truth.

8 I am the One source of all: the evolution of all comes from me. The wise think this and they worship me in adoration of love.

9 Their thoughts are on me, their life is in me, and they give light to each other. For ever they speak of my glory; and they find peace and joy.

10 To those who are ever in harmony, and who worship me with their love, I give the Yoga of vision and with this they come to me.

11 In my mercy I dwell in their hearts and I dispel their darkness of ignorance by the light of the lamp of wisdom.

ARJUNA

12 Supreme Brahman, Light supreme, and supreme purification, Spirit divine eternal, unborn God from the beginning, omnipresent Lord of all.

13 Thus all the seers praised thee: the seer divine Narada; Asita, Devala and Vyasa. And this is now thy revelation.

14 I have faith in all thy words, because these words are words of truth, and neither the gods in heaven nor the demons in hell can grasp thy infinite vastness.

15 Only thy Spirit knows thy Spirit: only thou knowest thyself. Source of Being in all beings, God of gods, ruler of all.

16 Tell me in thy mercy of thy divine glory wherein thou art ever, and all the worlds are.

17 For ever in meditation, how shall I ever know thee? And in what manifestations shall I think of thee, my Lord?

18 Speak to me again in full of thy power and of thy glory, for I am never tired, never, of hearing thy words of life.

KRISHNA

19 Listen and I shall reveal to thee some manifestations of my divine glory. Only the greatest, Arjuna, for there is no end to my infinite greatness.

20 I am the soul, prince victorious, which dwells in the heart of all things. I am the beginning, the middle, and the end of all that lives.

21 Among the sons of light I am Vishnu, and of luminaries the radiant sun. I am the lord of the winds and storms, and of the lights in the night I am the moon.

22 Of the Vedas I am the Veda of songs, and I am Indra, the chief of the gods. Above man's senses I am the mind, and in all living beings I am the light of consciousness.

23 Among the terrible powers I am the god of destruction; and among monsters Vittesa, the lord of wealth. Of radiant spirits I am fire; and among high mountains the mountain of the gods.

24 Of priests I am the divine priest Brihaspati, and among warriors Skanda, the god of war. Of lakes I am the vast ocean.

25 Among great seers I am Bhrigu; and of words I am OM, the Word of Eternity. Of prayers I am the prayer of silence; and of things that move not I am the Himalayas.

26 Of trees I am the tree of life, and of heavenly seers Narada. Among celestial musicians, Chitra-ratha; and among seers on earth, Kapila.

27 Of horses I am the horse of Indra, and of elephants his elephant Airavata. Among men I am king of men.

28 Of weapons I am the thunderbolt, and of cows the cow of wonder. Among creators I am the creator of love; and among serpents the serpent of Eternity.

29 Among the snakes of mystery I am Ananta, and of those born in the waters I am Varuna, their lord. Of the spirits of the fathers I am Aryaman, and of rulers Yama, the ruler of death.

30 Of demons I am Prahlada their prince, and of all things that measure I am time. Of beasts I am the king of beasts, and of birds Vainateya who carries a god.

31 Among things of purification I am the wind, and among warriors I am Rama, the hero supreme. Of fishes in the sea I am Makara the wonderful, and among all rivers the holy Ganges.

32 I am the beginning and the middle and the end of all that

is. Of all knowledge I am the knowledge of the Soul. Of the many paths of reason I am the one that leads to Truth.

33 Of sounds I am the first sound, A; of compounds I am co-ordination. I am time, never-ending time. I am the Creator who sees all.

34 I am death that carries off all things, and I am the source of things to come. Of feminine nouns I am Fame and Prosperity; Speech, Memory and Intelligence; Constancy and patient Forgiveness.

35 I am the Brihat songs of all songs in the Vedas. I am the Gayatri of all measures in verse. Of months I am the first of the year, and of the seasons the season of flowers.

36 I am the cleverness in the gambler's dice. I am the beauty of all things beautiful. I am victory and the struggle for victory. I am the goodness of those who are good.

37 Of the children of Vrishni I am Krishna; and of the sons of Pandu I am Arjuna. Among seers in silence I am Vyasa; and among poets the poet Usana.

38 I am the sceptre of the rulers of men; and I am the wise policy of those who seek victory. I am the silence of hidden mysteries; and I am the knowledge of those who know.

39 And know, Arjuna, that I am the seed of all things that are; and that no being that moves or moves not can ever be without me.

40 There is no end of my divine greatness, Arjuna. What I

have spoken here to thee shows only a small part of my Infinity.

41 Know thou that whatever is beautiful and good, whatever has glory and power is only a portion of my own radiance.

42 But of what help is it to thee to know this diversity? Know that with one single fraction of my Being I pervade and support the Universe, and know that I AM.

11

ARJUNA

1 In thy mercy thou hast told me the secret supreme of thy Spirit, and thy words have dispelled my delusion.

2 I have heard in full from thee of the coming and going of beings, and also of thy infinite greatness.

3 I have heard thy words of truth, but my soul is yearning to see: to see thy form as God of this all.

4 If thou thinkest, O my Lord, that it can be seen by me, show me, O God of Yoga, the glory of thine own Supreme Being.

KRISHNA

5 By hundreds and then by thousands, behold, Arjuna, my manifold celestial forms of innumerable shapes and colours.

6 Behold the gods of the sun, and those of fire and light; the gods of storm and lightning, and the two luminous charioteers of heaven. Behold, descendant of Bharata, marvels never seen before.

7 See now the whole universe with all things that move and

move not, and whatever thy soul may yearn to see. See it all as One in me.

8 But thou never canst see me with these thy mortal eyes: I will give thee divine sight. Behold my wonder and glory.

SANJAYA

9 When Krishna, the God of Yoga, had thus spoken, O king, he appeared then to Arjuna in his supreme divine form.

10 And Arjuna saw in that form countless visions of wonder: eyes from innumerable faces, numerous celestial ornaments, numberless heavenly weapons;

11 Celestial garlands and vestures, forms anointed with heavenly perfumes. The Infinite Divinity was facing all sides, all marvels in him containing.

12 If the light of a thousand suns suddenly arose in the sky, that splendour might be compared to the radiance of the Supreme Spirit.

13 And Arjuna saw in that radiance the whole universe in its variety, standing in a vast unity in the body of the God of gods.

14 Trembling with awe and wonder, Arjuna bowed his head, and joining his hands in adoration he thus spoke to his God.

15 I see in thee all the gods, O my God; and the infinity of the beings of thy creation. I see god Brahma on his throne of lotus, and all the seers and serpents of light.

16 All around I behold thy Infinity: the power of thy innumerable arms, the visions from thy innumerable eyes, the words from thy innumerable mouths, and the fire of life of thy innumerable bodies. Nowhere I see a beginning or middle or end of thee, O God of all, Form Infinite!

17 I see the splendour of an infinite beauty which illumines the whole universe. It is thee! with thy crown and sceptre and circle. How difficult thou art to see! But I see thee: as fire, as the sun, blinding, incomprehensible.

18 Thou art the Imperishable, the highest End of knowledge, the support of this vast universe. Thou, the everlasting ruler of the law of righteousness, the Spirit who is and who was at the beginning.

19 I see thee without beginning, middle, or end; I behold thy infinite power, the power of thy innumerable arms. I see thine eyes as the sun and the moon. And I see thy face as a sacred fire that gives light and life to the whole universe in the splendour of a vast offering.

20 Heaven and earth and all the infinite spaces are filled with thy Spirit; and before the wonder of thy fearful majesty the three worlds tremble.

21 The hosts of the gods come to thee and, joining palms in

awe and wonder, they praise and adore. Sages and saints come to thee, and praise thee with songs of glory.

22 The Rudras of destruction, the Vasus of fire, the Sadhyas of prayers, the Adityas of the sun; the lesser gods Visve-Devas, the two Asvins charioteers of heaven, the Maruts of winds and storms, the Ushmapas spirits of ancestors; the celestial choirs of Gandharvas, the Yakshas keepers of wealth, the demons of hell and the Siddhas who on earth reached perfection: they all behold thee with awe and wonder.

23 But the worlds also behold thy fearful mighty form, with many mouths and eyes, with many bellies, thighs and feet, frightening with terrible teeth: they tremble in fear, and I also tremble.

24 When I see thy vast form, reaching the sky, burning with many colours, with wide open mouths, with vast flaming eyes, my heart shakes in terror: my power is gone and gone is my peace, O Vishnu!

25 Like the fire at the end of Time which burns all in the last day, I see thy vast mouths and thy terrible teeth. Where am I? Where is my shelter? Have mercy on me, God of gods, Refuge Supreme of the world!

26 The sons of Dhrita-rashtra, all of them, with other prin-

27 ces of this earth, and Bhishma and Drona and great Karna, and also the greatest warriors of our host, all enter rushing into thy mouths, terror-inspiring with their

fearful fangs. Some are caught between them, and their heads crushed into powder.

28 As roaring torrents of waters rush forward into the ocean, so do these heroes of our mortal world rush into thy flaming mouths.

29 And as moths swiftly rushing enter a burning flame and die, so all these men rush to thy fire, rush fast to their own destruction.

30 The flames of thy mouths devour all the worlds. Thy glory fills the whole universe. But how terrible thy splendours burn!

31 Reveal thyself to me! Who art thou in this form of terror? I adore thee, O god supreme: be gracious unto me. I yearn to know thee, who art from the beginning: for I understand not thy mysterious works.

KRISHNA

32 I am all-powerful Time which destroys all things, and I have come here to slay these men. Even if thou dost not fight, all the warriors facing thee shall die.

33 Arise therefore! Win thy glory, conquer thine enemies, and enjoy thy kingdom. Through the fate of their Karma I have doomed them to die: be thou merely the means of my work.

34 Drona, Bhishma, Jayad-ratha and Karna, and other heroic warriors of this great war have already been slain by me: tremble not, fight and slay them. Thou shalt conquer thine enemies in battle.

SANJAYA

35 When Arjuna heard the words of Krishna he folded his hands trembling; and with a faltering voice, and bowing in adoration, he spoke.

ARJUNA

36 It is right, O God, that peoples sing thy praises, and that they are glad and rejoice in thee. All evil spirits fly away in fear; but the hosts of the saints bow down before thee.

37 How could they not bow down in love and adoration, before thee, God of gods, Spirit Supreme? Thou creator of Brahma, the god of creation, thou infinite, eternal, refuge of the world! Thou who art all that is, and all that is not, and all that is Beyond.

38 Thou God from the beginning, God in man since man was. Thou Treasure supreme of this vast universe. Thou the One to be known and the Knower, the final resting place. Thou infinite Presence in whom all things are.

39 God of the winds and the waters, of fire and death! Lord of the solitary moon, the Creator, the Ancestor of all! Adoration unto thee, a thousand adorations; and again and again unto thee adoration.

40 Adoration unto thee who art before me and behind me: adoration unto thee who art on all sides, God of all. All-powerful God of immeasurable might. Thou art the consummation of all: thou art all.

41 If in careless presumption, or even in friendliness, I said 'Krishna! Son of Yadu! My friend!', this I did unconscious of thy greatness.

42 And if in irreverence I was disrespectful—when alone or with others—and made a jest of thee at games, or resting, or at a feast, forgive me in thy mercy, O thou Immeasurable!

43 Father of all. Master supreme. Power supreme in all the worlds. Who is like thee? Who is beyond thee?

44 I bow before thee, I prostrate in adoration; and I beg thy grace, O glorious Lord! As a father to his son, as a friend to his friend, as a lover to his beloved, be gracious unto me, O God.

45 In a vision I have seen what no man has seen before: I rejoice in exultation, and yet my heart trembles with fear. Have mercy upon me, Lord of gods, Refuge of the whole universe: show me again thine own human form.

46 I yearn to see thee again with thy crown and sceptre and

circle. Show thyself to me again in thine own four-armed form, thou of arms infinite, Infinite Form.

47 By my grace and my wondrous power I have shown to thee, Arjuna, this form supreme made of light, which is the Infinite, the All: mine own form from the beginning, never seen by man before.

48 Neither Vedas, nor sacrifices, nor studies, nor benefactions, nor rituals, nor fearful austerities can give the vision of my Form Supreme. Thou alone hast seen this Form, thou the greatest of the Kurus.

49 Thou hast seen the tremendous form of my greatness, but fear not, and be not bewildered. Free from fear and with a glad heart see my friendly form again.

50 Thus spoke Vasudeva to Arjuna, and revealed himself in his human form. The God of all gave peace to his fears and showed himself in his peaceful beauty.

ARJUNA

51 When I see thy gentle human face, Krishna, I return to my own nature, and my heart has peace.

KRISHNA

52 Thou hast seen now face to face my form divine so hard to see: for even the gods in heaven ever long to see what thou hast seen.

53 Not by the Vedas, or an austere life, or gifts to the poor, or ritual offerings can I be seen as thou hast seen me.

54 Only by love can men see me, and know me, and come unto me.

55 He who works for me, who loves me, whose End Supreme I am, free from attachment to all things, and with love for all creation, he in truth comes unto me.

12

ARJUNA

1 Those who in oneness worship thee as God immanent in all; and those who worship the Transcendent, the Imperishable—Of these, who are the best Yogis?

KRISHNA

2 Those who set their hearts on me and ever in love worship me, and who have unshakable faith, these I hold as the best Yogis.

3 But those who worship the Imperishable, the Infinite, the Transcendent unmanifested; the Omnipresent, the Beyond all thought, the Immutable, the Neverchanging, the Ever One;

4 Who have all the powers of their soul in harmony, and the same loving mind for all; who find joy in the good of all beings—they reach in truth my very self.

5 Yet greater is the toil of those whose minds are set on the Transcendent, for the path of the Transcendent is hard for mortals to attain.

6 But they for whom I am the End Supreme, who surrender

7 all their works to me, and who with pure love meditate on me and adore me—these I very soon deliver from the ocean of death and life-in-death, because they have set their heart on me.

8 Set thy heart on me alone, and give to me thy understanding: thou shalt in truth live in me hereafter.

9 But if thou art unable to rest thy mind on me, then seek to reach me by the practice of Yoga concentration.

10 If thou art not able to practise concentration, consecrate all thy work to me. By merely doing actions in my service thou shalt attain perfection.

11 And if even this thou art not able to do, then take refuge in devotion to me and surrender to me the fruit of all thy work—with the selfless devotion of a humble heart.

12 For concentration is better than mere practice, and meditation is better than concentration; but higher than meditation is surrender in love of the fruit of one's actions, for on surrender follows peace.

13 The man who has a good will for all, who is friendly and has compassion; who has no thoughts of 'I' or 'mine', whose peace is the same in pleasures and sorrows, and who is forgiving;

14 This Yogi of union, ever full of my joy, whose soul is in harmony and whose determination is strong; whose mind and inner vision are set on me—this man loves me, and he is dear to me.

15 He whose peace is not shaken by others, and before whom other people find peace, beyond excitement and anger and fear—he is dear to me.

16 He who is free from vain expectations, who is pure, who is wise and knows what to do, who in inner peace watches both sides, who shakes not, who works for God and not for himself—this man loves me, and he is dear to me.

17 He who feels neither excitement nor repulsion, who complains not and lusts not for things; who is beyond good and evil, and who has love—he is dear to me.

18 The man whose love is the same for his enemies or his friends, whose soul is the same in honour or disgrace, who is beyond heat or cold or pleasure or pain, who is free from the chains of attachments;

19 Who is balanced in blame and in praise, whose soul is silent, who is happy with whatever he has, whose home is not in this world, and who has love—this man is dear to me.

20 But even dearer to me are those who have faith and love, and who have me as their End Supreme: those who hear my words of Truth, and who come to the waters of Everlasting Life.

13

KRISHNA

1 This body, Arjuna, is called the field. He who knows this is called the knower of the field.

2 Know that I am the knower in all the fields of my creation; and that the wisdom which sees the field and the knower of the field is true wisdom.

3 Hear from me briefly what the field is and how it is, what its changes are and whence each one comes; who is the knower and what is his power.

4 This has been sung by seers of the Vedas in many musical measures of verse; and in great words about Brahman, words of faith and full of truth.

5 The five elements, the thought of 'I', consciousness, sub-consciousness, the five powers of feeling and the five of action, the one mind over them, the five fields of sense-perception;

6 Desire, aversion, pleasure, pain, the power of mental unification, intelligence, and courage: this is the field and its modifications.

7 Humbleness, sincerity, harmlessness, forgiveness, uprightness, devotion to the spiritual master, purity, steadiness, self-harmony;

8 Freedom from the lust of the senses, absence of the thought of 'I', perception of the sorrows of birth, death, old age, disease, and suffering;

9 Freedom from the chains of attachments, even from a selfish attachment to one's children, wife, or home; an ever-present evenness of mind in pleasant or unpleasant events;

10 A single oneness of pure love, of never-straying love for me; retiring to solitary places, and avoiding the noisy multitudes;

11 A constant yearning to know the inner Spirit, and a vision of Truth which gives liberation: this is true wisdom leading to vision. All against this is ignorance.

12 Now I shall tell thee of the End of wisdom. When a man knows this he goes beyond death. It is Brahman, beginningless, supreme: beyond what is and beyond what is not.

13 His hands and feet are everywhere, he has heads and mouths everywhere; he sees all, he hears all. He is in all, and he is.

14 The Light of consciousness comes to him through infinite powers of perception, and yet he is above all these powers. He is beyond all, and yet he supports all. He is beyond the world of matter, and yet he has joy in this world.

15 He is invisible: he cannot be seen. He is far and he is

near, he moves and he moves not, he is within all and he is outside all.

16 He is ONE in all, but it seems as if he were many. He supports all beings: from him comes destruction, and from him comes creation.

17 He is the Light of all lights which shines beyond all darkness. It is vision, the end of vision, to be reached by vision, dwelling in the heart of all.

18 I have told thee briefly what is the field, what is wisdom, and what is the End of man's vision. When a man knows this he enters into my Being.

19 Know that Prakriti, Nature, and Purusha, Spirit, are both without beginning, and that temporal changes and Gunas, conditions, come all from nature.

20 Nature is the source of all material things: the maker, the means of making, and the thing made. Spirit is the source of all consciousness which feels pleasure and feels pain.

21 The spirit of man when in nature feels the ever-changing conditions of nature. When he binds himself to things ever-changing, a good or evil fate whirls him round through life-in-death.

22 But the Spirit Supreme in man is beyond fate. He watches, gives blessing, bears all, feels all. He is called the Lord Supreme and the Supreme Soul.

23 He who knows in truth this Spirit and knows nature with

23

its changing conditions, wherever this man may be he is no more whirled round by fate.

24 Some by the Yoga of meditation, and by the grace of the Spirit, see the Spirit in themselves; some by the Yoga of the vision of Truth; and others by the Yoga of work.

25 And yet there are others who do not know, but they hear from others and adore. They also cross beyond death, because of their devotion to words of Truth.

26 Whatever is born, Arjuna, whether it moves or it moves Not, know that it comes from the union of the field and the knower of the field.

27 He who sees that the Lord of all is ever the same in all that is, immortal in the field of mortality—he sees the truth.

28 And when a man sees that the God in himself is the same God in all that is, he hurts not himself by hurting others: then he goes indeed to the highest Path.

29 He who sees that all work, everywhere, is only the work of nature; and that the Spirit watches this work—he sees the truth.

30 When a man sees that the infinity of various beings is abiding in the ONE, and is an evolution from the ONE, then he becomes one with Brahman.

31 Beginningless and free from changing conditions, imperishable is the Spirit Supreme. Though he is in the body,

not his is the work of the body, and he is pure from the imperfection of all work.

32 Just as the omnipresent ether is pure because intangible, so the Spirit dwelling in matter is pure from the touch of matter.

33 And even as one sun gives light to all things in this world, so the Lord of the field gives light to all his field.

34 Those who with the eye of inner vision see the distinction between the field and the knower of the field, and see the liberation of spirit from matter, they go into the Supreme.

14

KRISHNA

1 I will reveal again a supreme wisdom, of all wisdom the highest: sages who have known it have gone hence to supreme perfection.

2 Taking refuge in this wisdom they have become part of me: they are not reborn at the time of creation, and they are not destroyed at the time of dissolution.

3 In the vastness of my Nature I place the seed of things to come; and from this union comes the birth of all beings.

4 Wherever a being may be born, Arjuna, know that my Nature is his mother and that I am the Father who gave him life.

5 SATTVA, RAJAS, TAMAS—light, fire, and darkness—are the three constituents of nature. They appear to limit in finite bodies the liberty of their infinite Spirit.*

6 Of these Sattva because it is pure, and it gives light and

---

*SATTVA, RAJAS, and TAMAS are the three 'Gunas', or the three 'strands' which, intertwined, are both the constituents and the changing conditions of nature. They are the light and harmony of pure intelligence and goodness; the fire and desire of impure mental energy and restless passion; and the darkness of dullness and inertia. Until final freedom is attained, they are clouds of matter darkening the Sun of the Spirit.

is the health of life, binds to earthly happiness and to lower knowledge.

7 Rajas is of the nature of passion, the source of thirst and attachment. It binds the soul of man to action.

8 Tamas, which is born of ignorance, darkens the soul of all men. It binds them to sleepy dullness, and then they do not watch and then they do not work.

9 Sattva binds to happiness; Rajas to action; Tamas, over-clouding wisdom, binds to lack of vigilance.

10 Sometimes Sattva may prevail over Rajas and Tamas, at others Rajas over Tamas and Sattva, and at others Tamas over Sattva and Rajas.

11 When the light of wisdom shines from the portals of the body's dwelling, then we know that Sattva is in power.

12 Greed, busy activity, many undertakings, unrest, the lust of desire—these arise when Rajas increases.

13 Darkness, inertia, negligence, delusion—these appear when Tamas prevails.

14 If the soul meets death when Sattva prevails, then it goes to the pure regions of those who are seeking Truth.

15 If a man meets death in a state of Rajas, he is reborn amongst those who are bound by their restless activity; and if he dies in Tamas he is reborn in the wombs of the irrational.

16 Any work when it is well done bears the pure harmony

of Sattva; but when done in Rajas it brings pain, and when done in Tamas it brings ignorance.

17 From Sattva arises wisdom, from Rajas greed, from Tamas negligence, delusion and ignorance.

18 Those who are in Sattva climb the path that leads on high, those who are in Rajas follow the level path, those who are in Tamas sink downwards on the lower path.

19 When the man of vision sees that the powers of nature are the only actors of this vast drama, and he beholds THAT which is beyond the powers of nature then he comes into my Being.

20 And when he goes beyond the three conditions of nature which constitute his mortal body then, free from birth, old age, and death, and sorrow, he enters into Immortality.

ARJUNA

21 How is the man known who has gone beyond the three powers of nature? What is his path; and how does he transcend the three?

22 He who hates not light, nor busy activity, nor even darkness, when they are near, neither longs for them when they are far;

23 Who unperturbed by changing conditions sits apart and watches and says 'the powers of nature go round', and remains firm and shakes not;

24 Who dwells in his inner self, and is the same in pleasure and pain; to whom gold or stones or earth are one, and what is pleasing or displeasing leave him in peace; who is beyond both praise and blame, and whose mind is steady and quiet;

25 Who is the same in honour or disgrace, and has the same love for enemies or friends, who surrenders all selfish undertakings—this man has gone beyond the three.

26 And he who with never-failing love adores me and works for me, he passes beyond the three powers and can be one with Brahman, the ONE.

27 For I am the abode of Brahman, the never-failing fountain of everlasting life. The law of righteousness is my law; and my joy is infinite joy.

15

KRISHNA

1 There is a tree, the tree of Transmigration, the Asvattha tree everlasting. Its roots are above in the Highest, and its branches are here below. Its leaves are sacred songs, and he who knows them knows the Vedas.

2 Its branches spread from earth to heaven, and the powers of nature give them life. Its buds are the pleasures of the senses. Far down below, its roots stretch into the world of men, binding a mortal through selfish actions.

3 Men do not see the changing form of that tree, nor its
4 beginning, nor its end, nor where its roots are. But let the wise see, and with the strong sword of dispassion let him cut this strong-rooted tree, and seek that path wherefrom those who go never return. Such a man can say: 'I go for refuge to that Eternal Spirit from whom the stream of creation came at the beginning.'

5 Because the man of pure vision, without pride or delusion, in liberty from the chains of attachments, with his soul ever in his inner Spirit, all selfish desires gone, and free from the two contraries known as pleasure and pain, goes to the abode of Eternity.

6 There the sun shines not, nor the moon gives light, nor

fire burns, for the Light of my glory is there. Those who reach that abode return no more.

7 A spark of my eternal Spirit becomes in this world a living soul; and this draws around its centre the five senses and the mind resting in nature.

8 When the Lord of the body arrives, and when he departs and wanders on, he takes them over with him, as the wind takes perfumes from their place of sleep.

9 And he watches over the mind and its senses—ear, eye, touch, and taste, and smell—and his consciousness enjoys their world.

10 When he departs, or when he stays, and with the powers of his nature enjoys life, those in delusion see him not, but he who has the eye of wisdom sees.

11 Seekers of union, ever striving, see him dwelling in their own hearts; but those who are not pure and have not wisdom, though they strive, never see him.

12 That splendour of light that comes from the sun and which illumines the whole universe, the soft light of the moon, the brightness of fire—know that they all come from me.

13 I come into the earth and with life-giving love I support all things on earth. And I become the scent and taste of the sacred plant Soma, which is the wandering moon.

14 I become the fire of life which is in all things that

breathe; and in union with the breath that flows in and flows out I burn the four kinds of food.

15 And I am in the heart of all. With me come memory and wisdom, and without me they depart. I am the knower and the knowledge of the Vedas, and the creator of their end, the Vedanta.

16 There are two spirits in this universe, the perishable and the imperishable. The perishable is all things in creation. The imperishable is that which moves not.

17 But the highest spirit is another: it is called the Spirit Supreme. He is the God of Eternity who pervading all sustains all.

18 Because I am beyond the perishable, and even beyond the imperishable, in this world and in the Vedas I am known as the Spirit Supreme.

19 He who with a clear vision sees me as the Spirit Supreme he knows all there is to be known, and he adores me with all his soul.

20 I have revealed to thee the most secret doctrine, Arjuna. He who sees it has seen light, and his task in this world is done.

16

KRISHNA

1 Freedom from fear, purity of heart, constancy in sacred learning and contemplation, generosity, self-harmony, adoration, study of the scriptures, austerity, righteousness;

2 Non-violence, truth, freedom from anger, renunciation, serenity, aversion to fault-finding, sympathy for all beings, peace from greedy cravings, gentleness, modesty, steadiness;

3 Energy, forgiveness, fortitude, purity, a good will, freedom from pride—these are the treasures of the man who is born for heaven.

4 Deceitfulness, insolence and self-conceit, anger and harshness and ignorance—these belong to a man who is born for hell.

5 The virtues of heaven are for liberation but the sins of hell are the chains of the soul. Grieve not, Arjuna, for heaven is thy final end.

6 There are two natures in this world: the one is of heaven, the other of hell. The heavenly nature has been explained: hear now of the evil of hell.

7 Evil men know not what should be done or what should

not be done. Purity is not in their hearts, nor good conduct, nor truth.

8 They say: 'This world has no truth, no moral foundation, no God. There is no law of creation: what is the cause of birth but lust?'

9 Firm in this belief, these men of dead souls, of truly little intelligence, undertake their work of evil: they are the enemies of this fair world, working for its destruction.

10 They torture their soul with insatiable desires and full of deceit, insolence, and pride, they hold fast their dark ideas, and they carry on their impure work.

11 Thus they are beset with innumerable cares which last long, all their life, until death. Their highest aim is sensual enjoyment, and they firmly think that this is all.

12 They are bound by hundreds of vain hopes. Anger and lust is their refuge; and they strive by unjust means to amass wealth for their own cravings.

13 'I have gained this today, and I shall attain this desire. This wealth is mine, and that shall also be mine.'

14 'I have slain that enemy, and others also shall I slay. I am a lord, I enjoy life, I am successful, powerful and happy.'

15 'I am wealthy and of noble birth: who else is there like me? I shall pay for religious rituals, I shall make benefactions, I shall enjoy myself.' Thus they say in their darkness of delusion.

16 Led astray by many wrong thoughts, entangled in the net of delusion, enchained to the pleasures of their cravings, they fall down into a foul hell.

17 In their haughtiness of vainglory, drunk with the pride of their wealth, they offer their wrong sacrifices for ostentation, against divine law.

18 In their chains of selfishness and arrogance, of violence and anger and lust, these malignant men hate me: they hate me in themselves and in others.

19 In the vast cycles of life and death I inexorably hurl them down to destruction: these the lowest of men, cruel and evil, whose soul is hate.

20 Reborn in a lower life, in darkness birth after birth, they come not to me, Arjuna; but they go down the path of hell.

21 Three are the gates to this hell, the death of the soul: the gate of lust, the gate of wrath, and the gate of greed. Let a man shun the three.

22 When a man is free from these three doors of darkness, he does what is good for his soul, and then he enters the Path Supreme.

23 But the man who rejects the words of the Scriptures and follows the impulse of desire attains neither his perfection, nor joy, nor the Path Supreme.

24 Let the Scriptures be therefore thy authority as to what is

right and what is not right. Know the words of the Scriptures, and do in this life the work to be done.

ARJUNA

1 Those who forsake the law of the Scriptures and yet offer
sacrifice full of faith—What is their condition, Krishna?
Is it of Sattva, Rajas, or Tamas—of light, of fire, or of
darkness?

KRISHNA

2 The faith of men, born of their nature, is of three kinds:
of light, of fire and of darkness. Hear now of these.

3 The faith of a man follows his nature, Arjuna. Man is
made of faith: as his faith is so he is.

4 Men of light worship the gods of Light; men of fire worship the gods of power and wealth; men of darkness worship ghosts and spirits of night.

5 There are men selfish and false who moved by their lusts
6 and passions perform terrible austerities not ordained by
sacred books: fools who torture the powers of life in their
bodies and me who dwells in them. Know that their mind
is darkness.

7 Hear now of three kinds of food, the three kinds of sac-

rifice, the three kinds of harmony, and the three kinds of gifts.

8 Men who are pure like food which is pure: which gives health, mental power, strength and long life; which has taste, is soothing and nourishing, and which makes glad the heart of man.

9 Men of Rajas like food of Rajas: acid and sharp, and salty and dry, and which brings heaviness and sickness and pain.

10 Men of darkness eat food which is stale and tasteless, which is rotten and left over night, impure, unfit for holy offerings.

11 A sacrifice is pure when it is an offering of adoration in harmony with the holy law, with no expectation of a reward, and with the heart saying 'it is my duty'.

12 But a sacrifice that is done for the sake of a reward, or for the sake of vainglory is an impure sacrifice of Rajas.

13 And a sacrifice done against the holy law, without faith, and sacred words, and the gifts of food, and the due offering, is a sacrifice of darkness.

14 Reverence for the gods of Light, for the twice-born, for the teachers of the Spirit and for the wise; and also purity, righteousness, chastity and non-violence: this is the harmony of the body.

15 Words which give peace, words which are good and

beautiful and true, and also the reading of sacred books: this is the harmony of words.

16 Quietness of mind, silence, self-harmony, loving-kindness, and a pure heart: this is the harmony of the mind.

17 This threefold harmony is called pure when it is practised with supreme faith with no desire for a reward and with oneness of soul.

18 But false austerity, for the sake of reputation, honour and reverence, is impure: it belongs to Rajas and is unstable and uncertain.

19 When self-control is self-torture, due to dullness of the mind, or when it aims at hurting another, then self-control is of darkness.

20 A gift is pure when it is given from the heart to the right person at the right time and at the right place, and when we expect nothing in return.

21 But when it is given expecting something in return, or for the sake of a future reward, or when it is given unwillingly, the gift is of Rajas, impure.

22 And a gift given to the wrong person, at the wrong time and the wrong place, or a gift which comes not from the heart, and is given with proud contempt, is a gift of darkness.

23 OM, TAT, SAT. Each one of these three words is one word for Brahman, from whom came in the beginning the Brahmins, the Vedas and the Sacrifice.

24 Therefore with the word OM the lovers of Brahman begin all work of sacrifice, gift or self-harmony, done according to the Scriptures.

25 And with the word TAT, and with renunciation of all reward, this same work of sacrifice, gift or self-harmony is being done by those seekers of Infinite Liberty.

26 SAT is what is good and what is true: when therefore a work is well done the end of that work is SAT.

27 Constant faithfulness in sacrifice, gift, or self-harmony is SAT; and also all work consecrated to Brahman.

28 But work done without faith is ASAT, is nothing: sacrifice, gift, or self-harmony done without faith are nothing, both in this world and in the world to come.

18

ARJUNA

1 Speak to me, Krishna, of the essence of renunciation, and
of the essence of surrender.

KRISHNA

2 The renunciation of selfish works is called renunciation;
but the surrender of the reward of all work is called surrender.

3 Some say that there should be renunciation of action—
since action disturbs contemplation; but others say that
works of sacrifice, gift and self-harmony should not be
renounced.

4 Hear my truth about the surrender of works, Arjuna. Surrender, O best of men, is of three kinds.

5 Works of sacrifice, gift, and self-harmony should not be
abandoned, but should indeed be performed; for these
are works of purification.

6 But even these works, Arjuna, should be done in the freedom of a pure offering, and without expectation of a reward. This is my final word.

7 It is not right to leave undone the holy work which ought to be done. Such a surrender of action would be a delusion of darkness.

8 And he who abandons his duty because he has fear of pain, his surrender is of Rajas, impure, and in truth he has no reward.

9 But he who does holy work, Arjuna, because it ought to be done, and surrenders selfishness and thought of reward, his work is pure, and is peace.

10 This man sees and has no doubts: he surrenders, he is pure and has peace. Work, pleasant or painful, is for him joy.

11 For there is no man on earth who can fully renounce living work, but he who renounces the reward of his work is in truth a man of renunciation.

12 When work is done for a reward, the work brings pleasure, or pain, or both, in its time; but when a man does work in Eternity, then Eternity is his reward.

13 Know now from me, Arjuna, the five causes of all actions as given in the Sankhya wisdom, wherein is found the end of all works.

14 The body, the lower 'I am', the means of perception, the means of action, and Fate. These are the five.

15 Whatever a man does, good or bad, in thought, word or deed, has these five sources of action.

16 If one thinks that his infinite Spirit does the finite work which nature does, he is a man of clouded vision and he does not see the truth.

17 He who is free from the chains of selfishness, and whose mind is free from any ill-will, even if he kills all these warriors he kills them not and he is free.

18 In the idea of a work there is the knower, the knowing and the known. When the idea is work there is the doer, the doing and the thing done.

19 The knowing, the doer and the thing done are said in the science of the 'Gunas' to be of three kinds, according to their qualities. Hear of these three.

20 When one sees Eternity in things that pass away and Infinity in finite things, then one has pure knowledge.

21 But if one merely sees the diversity of things, with their divisions and limitations, then one has impure knowledge.

22 And if one selfishly sees a thing as if it were everything, independent of the ONE and the many, then one is in the darkness of ignorance.

23 When work is done as sacred work, unselfishly, with a peaceful mind, without lust or hate, with no desire for reward, then the work is pure.

24 But when work is done with selfish desire, or feeling it is an effort, or thinking it is a sacrifice, then the work is impure.

25 And that work which is done with a confused mind, without considering what may follow, or one's own powers, or the harm done to others, or one's own loss, is work of darkness.

26 A man free from the chains of selfish attachments, free from his lower 'I am', who has determination and perseverance, and whose inner peace is beyond victory or defeat—such a man has pure Sattva.

27 But a man who is a slave of his passions, who works for selfish ends, who is greedy, violent and impure, and who is moved by pleasure and pain, is a man of impure Rajas.

28 And a man without self-harmony, vulgar, arrogant and deceitful; malicious, indolent and despondent, and also procrastinating, is a man of the darkness of Tamas.

29 Hear now fully and in detail the threefold division of wisdom and steadiness, according to the three Gunas.

30 There is a wisdom which knows when to go and when to return, what is to be done and what is not to be done, what is fear and what is courage, what is bondage and what is liberation—that is pure wisdom.

31 Impure wisdom has no clear vision of what is right and what is wrong, what should be done and what should not be done.

32 And there is a wisdom obscured in darkness when wrong is thought to be right, and when things are thought to be that which they are not.

33 When in the Yoga of holy contemplation the movements of the mind and of the breath of life are in a harmony of peace, there is steadiness, and that steadiness is pure.

34 But that steadiness which, with a desire for rewards, attaches itself to wealth, pleasure, and even religious ritual, is a steadiness of passion, impure.

35 And that steadiness whereby a fool does not surrender laziness, fear, self-pity, depression and lust, is indeed a steadiness of darkness.

36 Hear now, great Arjuna, of the three kinds of pleasure. There is the pleasure of following that right path which leads to the end of all pain.

37 What seems at first a cup of sorrow is found in the end immortal wine. That pleasure is pure: it is the joy which arises from a clear vision of the Spirit.

38 But the pleasure which comes from the craving of the senses with the objects of their desire, which seems at first a drink of sweetness but is found in the end a cup of poison, is the pleasure of passion, impure.

39 And that pleasure which both in the beginning and in the end is only a delusion of the soul, which comes from the dullness of sleep, laziness or carelessness, is the pleasure of darkness.

40 There is nothing on earth or in heaven which is free from these three powers of Nature.

41 The works of Brahmins, Kshatriyas, Vaisyas and Sudras

are different, in harmony with the three powers of their born nature.

42 The works of a Brahmin are peace; self-harmony, austerity and purity; loving-forgiveness and righteousness; vision and wisdom and faith.

43 These are the works of a Kshatriya: a heroic mind, inner fire, constancy, resourcefulness, courage in battle, generosity and noble leadership.

44 Trade, agriculture and the rearing of cattle is the work of a Vaisya. And the work of the Sudra is service.

45 They all attain perfection when they find joy in their work. Hear how a man attains perfection and finds joy in his work.

46 A man attains perfection when his work is worship of God, from whom all things come and who is in all.

47 Greater is thine own work, even if this be humble, than the work of another, even if this be great. When a man does the work God gives him, no sin can touch this man.

48 And a man should not abandon his work, even if he cannot achieve it in full perfection; because in all work there may be imperfection, even as in all fire there is smoke.

49 When a man has his reason in freedom from bondage, and his soul is in harmony, beyond desires, then renunciation leads him to a region supreme which is beyond earthly action.

50 Hear now how he then reaches Brahman, the highest vision of Light.

51 When the vision of reason is clear, and in steadiness the soul is in harmony; when the world of sound and other senses is gone, and the spirit has risen above passion and hate;

52 When a man dwells in the solitude of silence, and meditation and contemplation are ever with him; when too much food does not disturb his health, and his thoughts and words and body are in peace; when freedom from passion is his constant will;

53 And his selfishness and violence and pride are gone; when lust and anger and greediness are no more, and he is free from the thought 'this is mine'; then this man has risen on the mountain of the Highest: he is worthy to be one with Brahman, with God.

54 He is one with Brahman, with God, and beyond grief and desire his soul is in peace. His love is one for all creation, and he has supreme love for me.

55 By love he knows me in truth, who I am and what I am. And when he knows me in truth he enters into my Being.

56 In whatever work he does he can take refuge in me, and he attains then by my grace the imperishable home of Eternity.

57 Offer in thy heart all thy works to me, and see me as the

End of thy love, take refuge in the Yoga of reason, and ever rest thy soul in me.

58 If thy soul finds rest in me, thou shalt overcome all dangers by my grace; but if thy thoughts are on thyself, and thou wilt not listen, thou shalt perish.

59 If thou wilt not fight thy battle of life because in selfishness thou art afraid of the battle, thy resolution is in vain: nature will compel thee.

60 Because thou art in the bondage of Karma, of the forces of thine own past life; and that which thou, in thy delusion, with a good will dost not want to do, unwillingly thou shalt have to do.

61 God dwells in the heart of all beings, Arjuna: thy God dwells in my heart. And his power of wonder moves all things—puppets in a play of shadows—whirling them onwards on the stream of time.

62 Go to him for thy salvation with all thy soul, victorious man. By his grace thou shalt obtain the peace supreme, thy home of Eternity.

63 I have given thee words of vision and wisdom more secret than hidden mysteries. Ponder them in the silence of thy soul, and then in freedom do thy will.

64 Hear again my Word supreme, the deepest secret of silence. Because I love thee well, I will speak to thee words of salvation.

65 Give thy mind to me, and give me thy heart, and thy sac-

rifice, and thy adoration. This is my Word of promise: thou shalt in truth come to me, for thou art dear to me.

66 Leave all things behind, and come to me for thy salvation. I will make thee free from the bondage of sins. Fear no more.

67 These things must never be spoken to one who lacks self-discipline, or who has no love, or who dos not want to hear or who argues against me.

68 But he who will teach this secret doctrine to those who have love for me, and who himself has supreme love, he in truth shall come unto me.

69 For there can be no man among men who does greater work for me, nor can there be a man on earth who is dearer to me than he is.

70 He who learns in contemplation the holy words of our discourse, the light of his vision is his adoration. This is my truth.

71 And he who only hears but has faith, and in his heart he has no doubts, he also attains liberation and the worlds of joy of righteous men.

72 Hast thou heard these words, Arjuna, in the silent communion of thy soul? Has the darkness of thy delusion been dispelled by thine inner Light?

ARJUNA

73 By thy grace I remember my Light, and now gone is my delusion. My doubts are no more, my faith is firm; and now I can say 'Thy will be done'.

SANJAYA

74 Thus I heard these words of glory between Arjuna and the God of all, and they fill my soul with awe and wonder

75 By the grace of the poet Vyasa I heard these words of secret silence. I heard the mystery of Yoga, taught by Krishna the Master himself.

76 I remember, O king, I remember the words of holy wonder between Krishna and Arjuna, and again and again my soul feels joy.

77 And I remember, I ever remember, that vision of glory of the God of all, and again and again joy fills my soul.

78 Wherever is Krishna, the End of Yoga, wherever is Arjuna who masters the bow, there is beauty and victory, and joy and all righteousness. This is my faith.

PENGUIN 60s CLASSICS

PENGUIN 60s CLASSICS

ANONYMOUS WORKS